MAMMALS

MAMMIFÈRES

SÄUGETIERE

MAMMIFERI

MAMÍFEROS

哺乳動物

動物版畫

MAMMALS

DOVER**PICTURA**

DOVER PUBLICATIONS, Inc. | Mineola, New York

Selected and designed by Thalia Large and Alan Weller.

Copyright © 2004 by Dover Publications, Inc.
Digital images copyright © 2004 by Dover Publications, Inc.
All rights reserved.

Mammals is a new work, first published by Dover Publications, Inc., in 2004.

The illustrations contained in this book and CD-ROM belong to the Dover Pictura Electronic Design Series. They are permission-free, and may be used as a graphic resource provided no more than ten images are included in the same publication or project. The use of any of these images in book, electronic, or any other format for resale or distribution as royalty-free graphics is strictly prohibited.

For permission to use more than ten images, please contact:
Permissions Department
Dover Publications, Inc.
31 East 2nd Street
Mineola, NY 11501
rights@doverpublications.com

The CD-ROM file names correspond to the images in the book. All of the artwork stored on the CD-ROM can be imported directly into a wide range of design and word-processing programs on either Windows or Macintosh platforms. No further installation is necessary.

International Standard Book Number: 0-486-99638-7

Manufactured in Hong Kong
Dover Publications, Inc., 31 East 2nd Street, Mineola, NY 11501
www.doverpublications.com

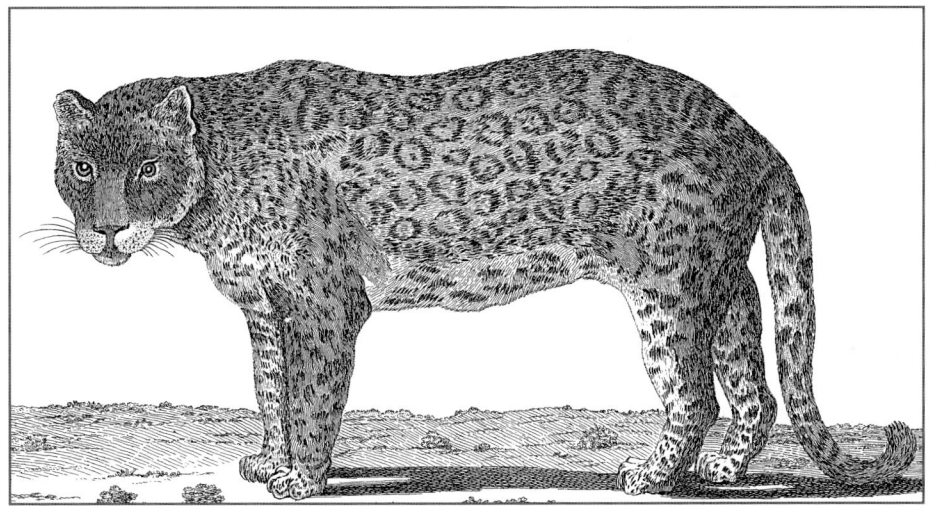

16–18

26

27

31

32

24

33

34

30 45, 46

50

51

52

53

54, 55

60

61

62

63

64

65

66

Echelle de 12 Pouces

68

72

73

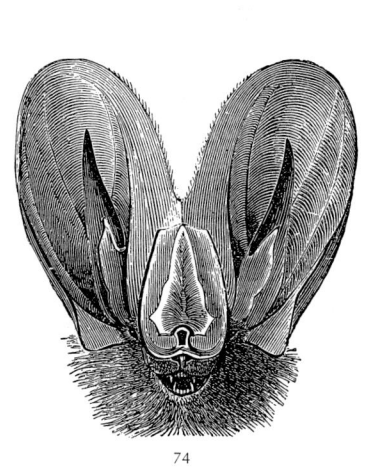
74

75

76

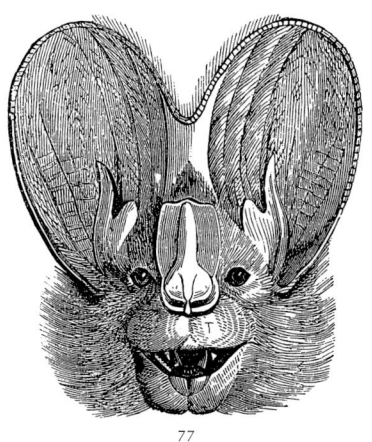
77

83

84

49

Fig. 4. Le Lerot à queue dorée.

86

90

94

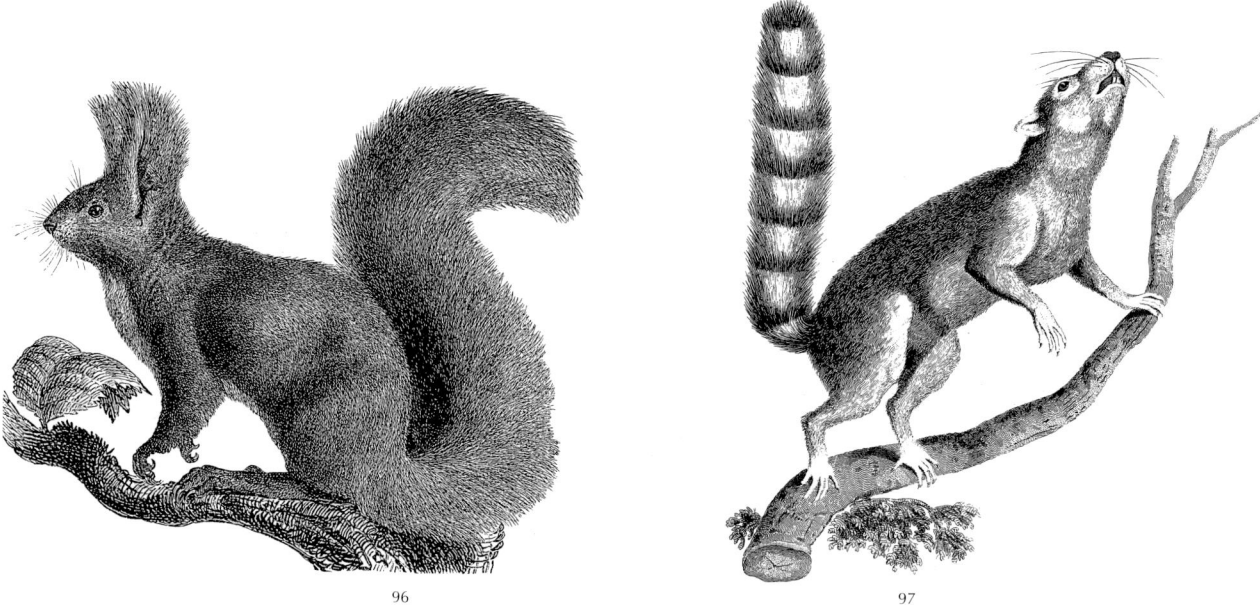

105

106

115

116

117

118–121   122–125   126–129

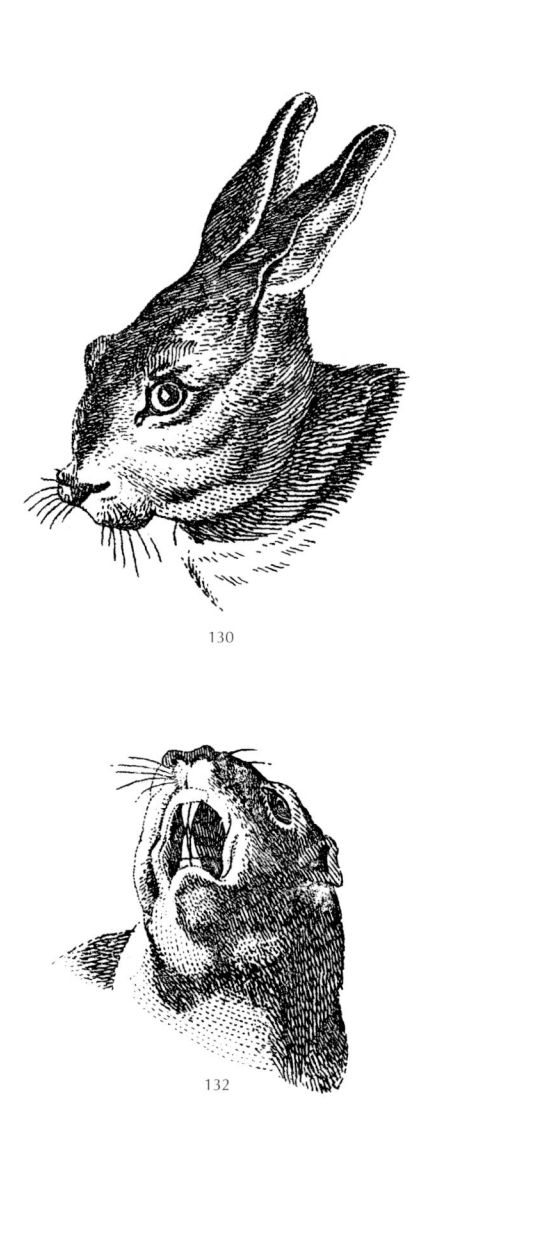

130

131

132

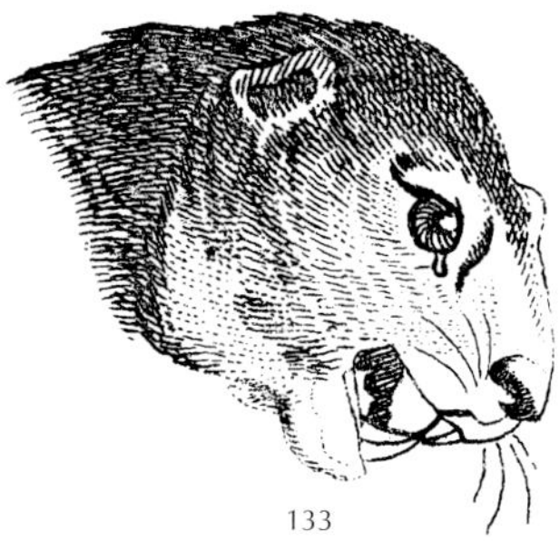

133

134

135

140

141

142

143

144

145

146

147

148

149

150

151

152

153

154

155

159

160

161

162

163

164

165

166

167

168

176

184

185

187

188

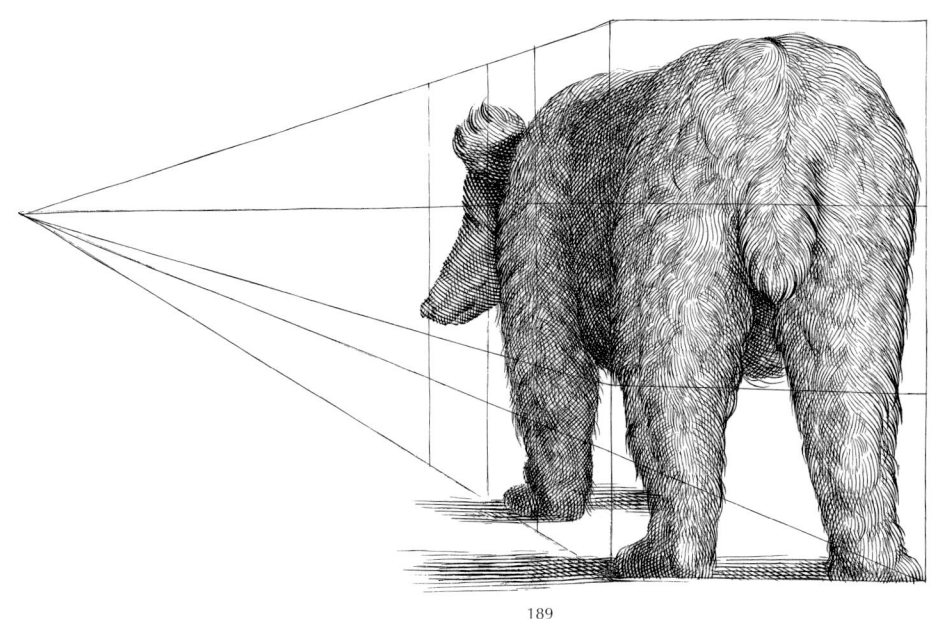
189

190

193

194

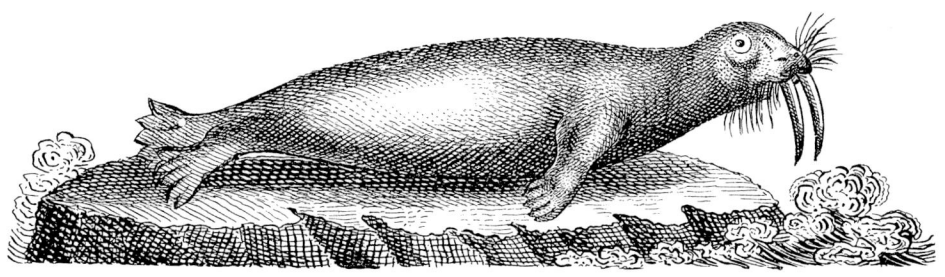

195

196

199

200

201

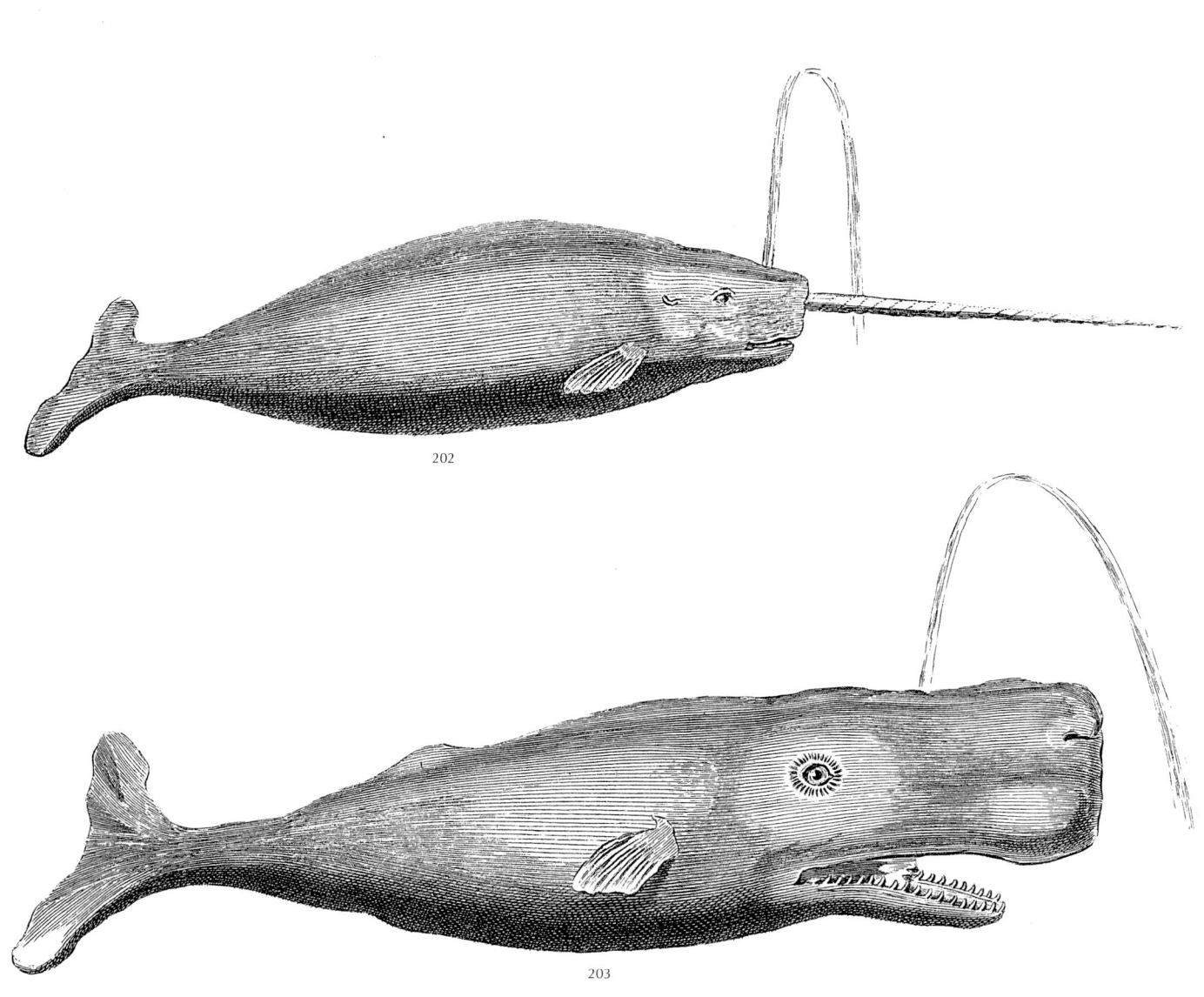

202

203

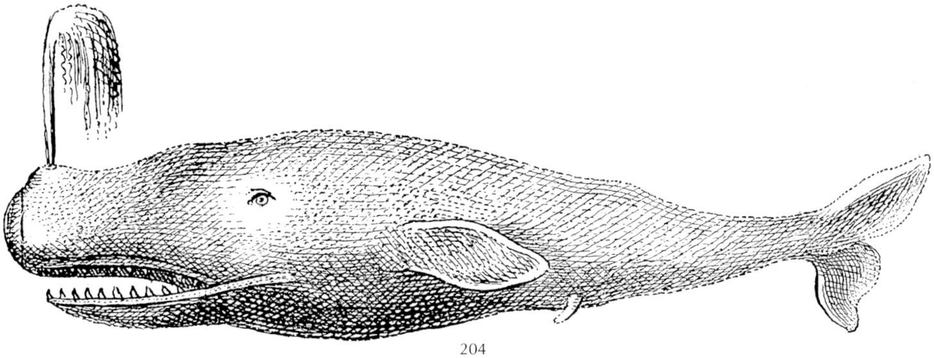

204

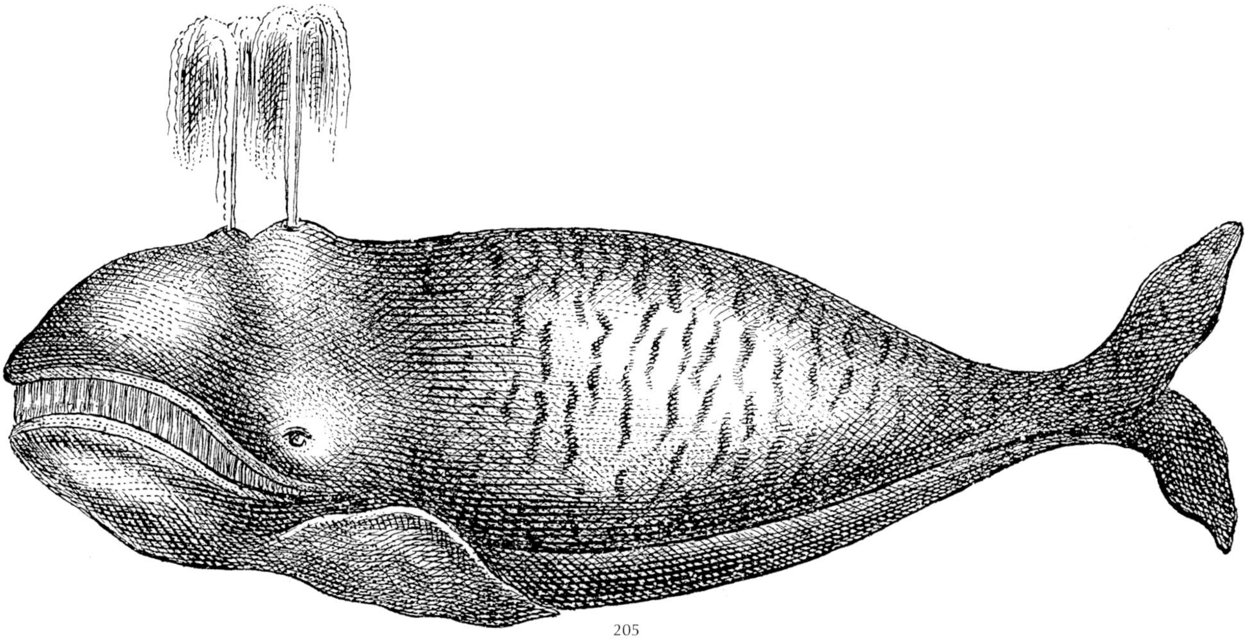

205

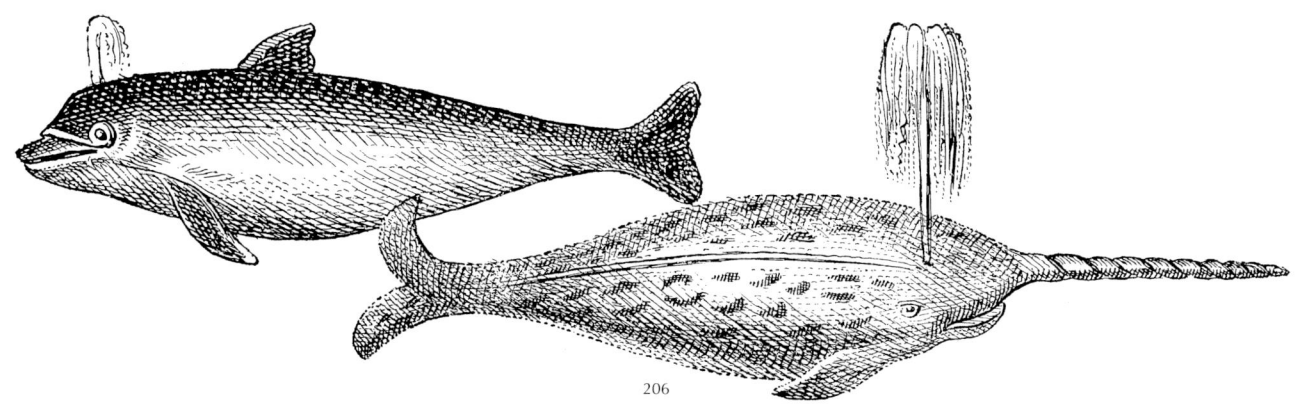
206

207

208

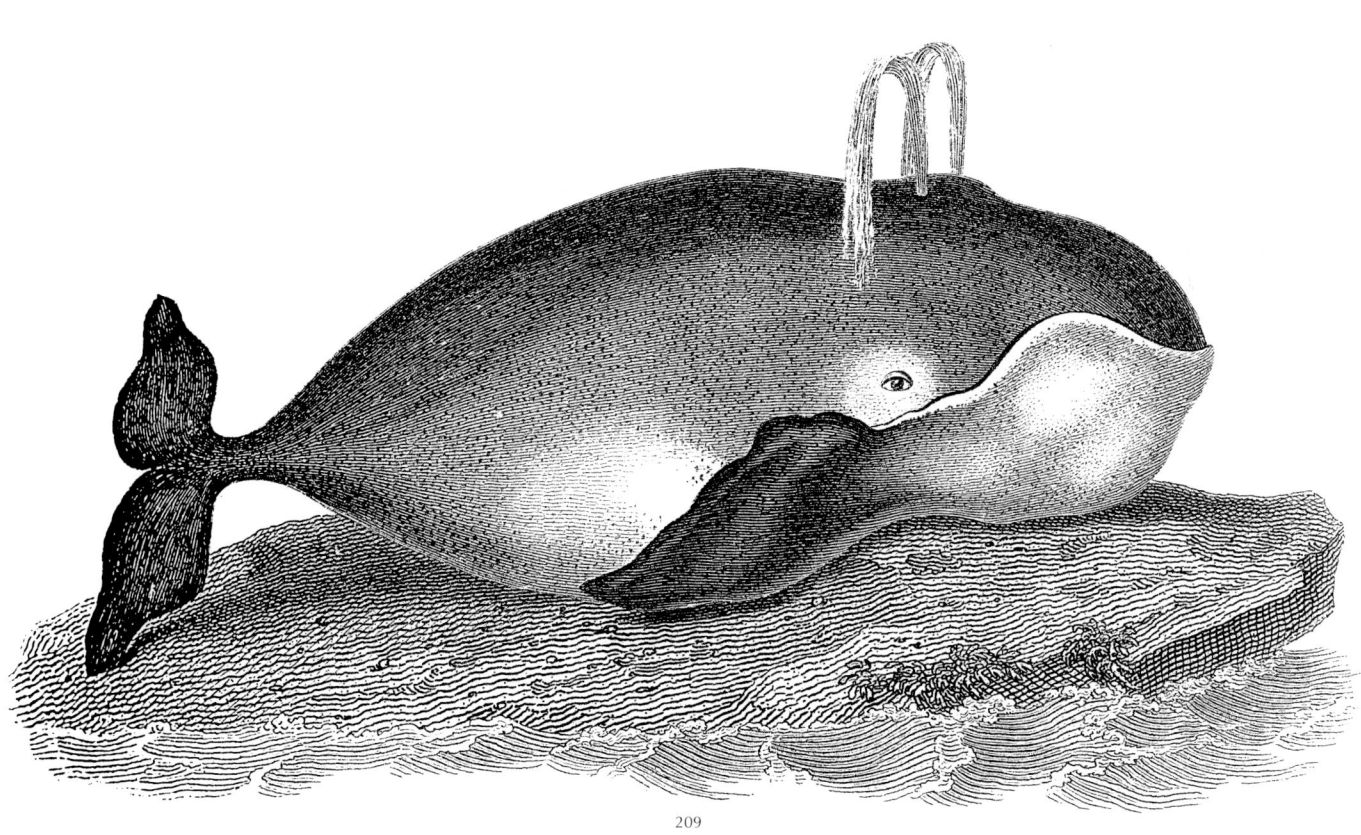

212

216

217

218

219

220

222

223

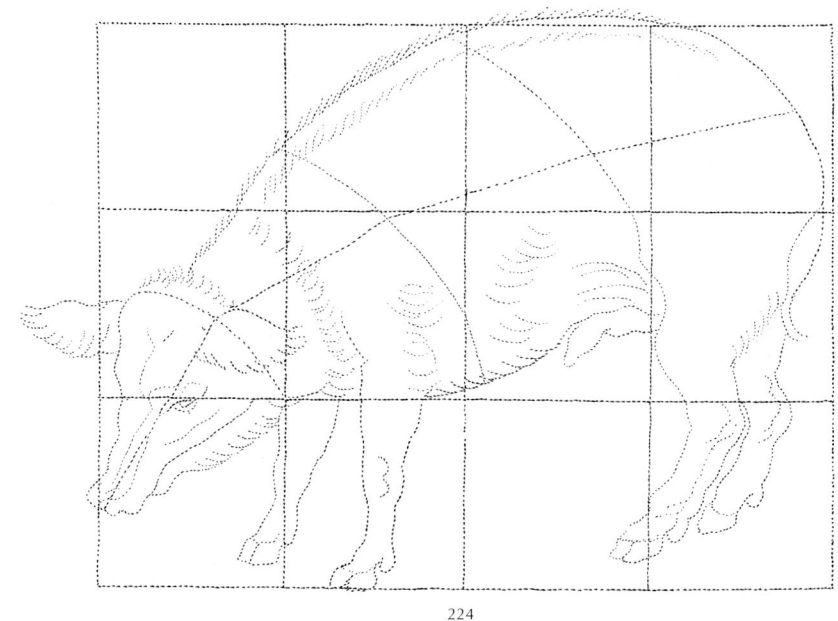
224

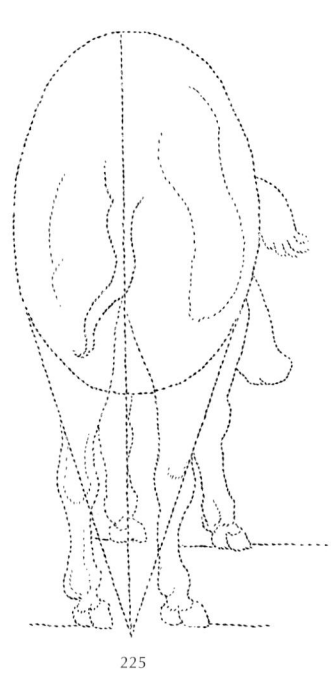
225

226

227

228

230

231

233

234

235

236

238

239

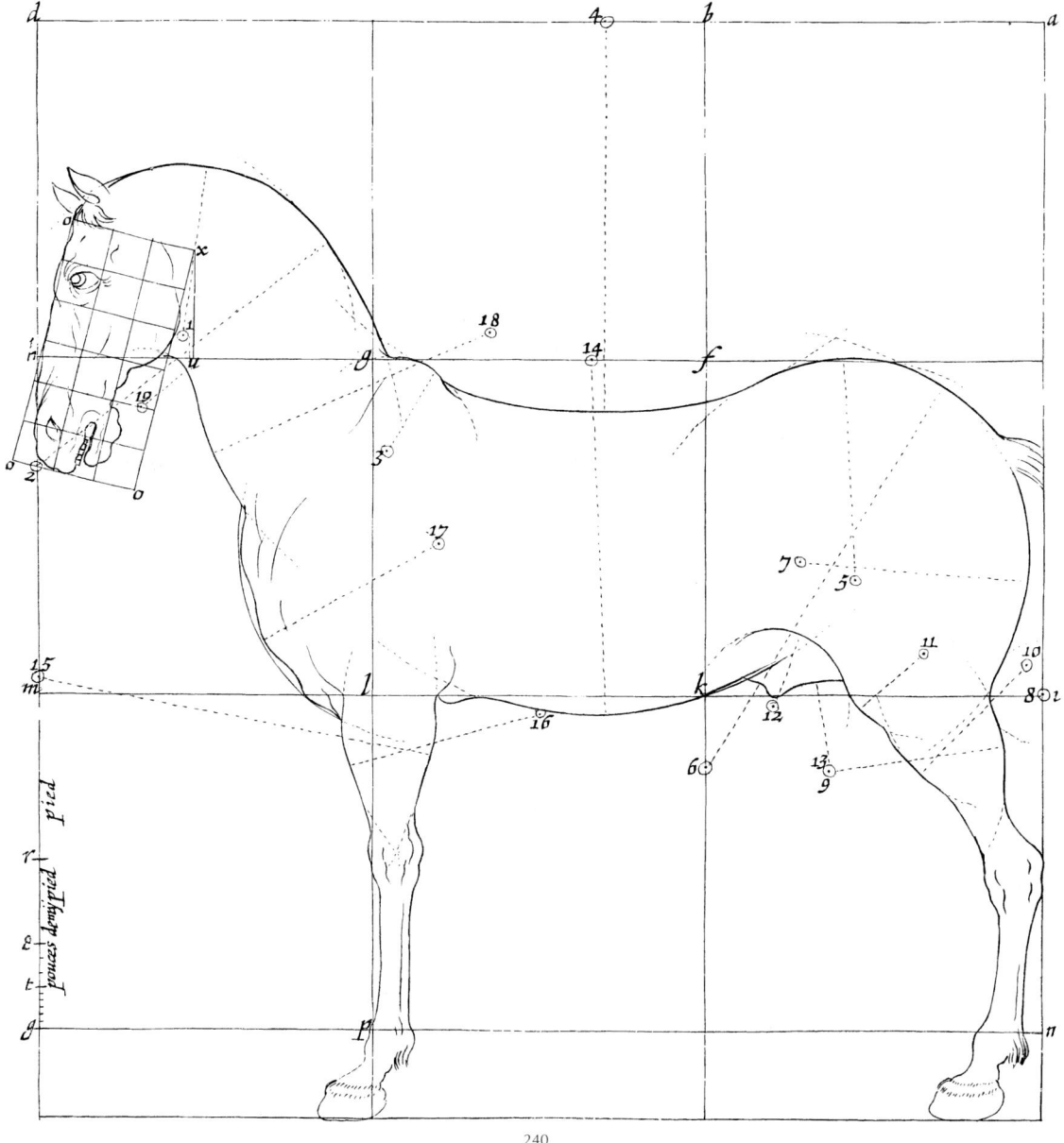

242

243

245